MADE FOR
more

An offer of hope and purpose

EMILY COBB

matthiasmedia

SYDNEY · YOUNGSTOWN

Made for More
© Emily Cobb 2018

Matthias Media
(St Matthias Press Ltd ACN 067 558 365)
Email: info@matthiasmedia.com.au
Internet: www.matthiasmedia.com.au
Please visit our website for current postal and telephone contact information.

Matthias Media (USA)
Email: sales@matthiasmedia.com
Internet: www.matthiasmedia.com
Please visit our website for current postal and telephone contact information.

Scripture taken from the Holy Bible, NEW INTERNATIONAL VERSION®, NIV®. Copyright © 1973, 1978, 1984, 2011 by Biblica, Inc. All rights reserved worldwide. Used by permission.

The quotation from CS Lewis in chapter 12 is taken from *The Weight of Glory* by CS Lewis, © copyright CS Lewis Pte Ltd 1949. Used with the kind permission of The CS Lewis Company.

ISBN 978 1 925424 24 9

Cover design by Emily Cobb and Lankshear Design.
Typesetting by Lankshear Design.

For Imogen, Gideon and Esther.
My deepest prayer is that you may seek and find
Jesus, the author of life.
And for David, my partner for the journey.
You always point me to Jesus. You make life
brighter and more fun.

Contents

1
On longing

It feels like it happened yesterday; stepping into the sunshine in my swimmers, self-consciously enveloped in my towel. I was 15 years old, and my swimming class had been combined with the boys' to perform some safety drills.

Living on the coast, swimming wasn't my issue. Being in a swimming costume was. Like any 'normal' person, I had hang-ups about my appearance. But my particular concern, on this particular afternoon, was my scoliosis—my spine wasn't straight. I'd learned to disguise it with clothes, but a swimming costume could not cover up the fact that one of my ribs stuck out the front, one protruded out the back, and my spine was doing the hula when it should have been doing a waltz.

As I walked to the line of students, knowing the moment would come when I had to drop my towel in front of my peers (including the guy I had a secret crush on), I felt a deep sense of longing. Longing to look more like the blonde beach babe. Longing to be sick or away that day. Longing to be loved completely by a guy who wanted me and no-one else—one who knew my hang-ups and came to love my body's hula over the usual waltz.

The years since this event have dimmed these particular hang-ups, but still this sense of longing lingers. Most of the time I don't notice it—as life has grown busier, responsibilities greater and I'm immersed in so much noise, my longings often get drowned out. Maybe that's true for you too; the busyness, the chaos and even the delights of life suppress any deep sense of a longing for more. But if we unplug for a moment, and press pause on the busy, what drives who we are? What deep burdens and desires of our heart bubble to the surface?

What do you *long* for?

I don't know if you grew up confident or resentful of your looks, if you had boyfriends or hopeless crushes, whether you hung out with the nerds or the cheerleaders. Were you the wallflower wishing to take part in the dance of life but fearing you didn't know the steps? As members of the human race, we all long for something. Recognized or not, there are things that fill our minds and take root in the depths of our hearts.

Longing for something

A few years ago, a friend introduced me to a German word: *Sehnsucht*. It doesn't have a direct English equivalent, but when we break it down into its parts we get a sense of its meaning. *Sehnen* means 'to yearn' and *sucht* describes 'an insatiable craving'. When it's applied to the human condition, the word implies incompleteness. It's reminiscent of the ancient Greek belief that every person has been separated into two souls and so spend their lives longing for their other half, their soul mate, until they meet them. It's the idea that we have longings that can be fulfilled only in relationships.

Author CS Lewis puts forward a different reason for the longing in every human heart. The reason our deepest desires or longings seem unable to be fulfilled is not because we have been separated from our other half, but because we were made for another world.[1] What we long for cannot be realized or met on this earth, because we were designed for a different world to the one we currently exist in. I don't mean that we were meant to be on a different planet—like when people say, "men are from Mars and women are from Venus". It comes instead from the idea that the world we live in isn't what it should be, and we long for something more.

Exploring our longing

I love the poem 'Journey to the Interior' by Margaret Atwood. In it, Atwood uses physical depictions of the Canadian landscape to describe an inner journey—one where we venture 'inside ourselves' to discover our motivations, dreams and hopes.

She compares this self-examination to a pioneer discovering uncharted territory. Like the towel that hid my swimmer-clad body, we hide facets of ourselves under a

---

1   CS Lewis, *Mere Christianity*, Harper Collins, New York, 2001, p. 138.

series of well-constructed layers. Atwood suggests that when we stop and go through a process of self-examination, we bravely navigate these layers, peeling them back and uncovering something precious.

If we were to explore this inner landscape, and took the time to look into who we are... what *longings* would we find? Like Atwood suggests, do we journey to our interior, recognizing the danger and challenge, but press on in spite of this, knowing that we can't process who we really are until we recognize what drives us? Or do we take the 'head in the sand' route, opting instead to ignore our longings and simply fill our lives with things that prevent us considering the deeper issues?

Sometimes we long for short-term things—like the latest iPhone, or the next episode of a show, or a piece of chocolate after a long, hard day. But don't you find that, as soon as you get your hands on one elusive thing, then a shallow longing for the next thing, and then the next thing, arises? For me, it becomes this perpetual cycle of cravings and unfulfilling fixes.

I think these short-term longings often disguise a deep-down, long-term longing in all of us—a longing for something more substantial than what the things in our world can offer. It's a scary thing to do, but if we look deep inside ourselves all of us would find there's a feeling that something may be missing—we can't necessarily put our finger on it, just an awareness there is something more to life that we are lacking.

Now, this may seem a little deep for the first chapter of a small book. And I would agree with you—it is deep, and this is a small book! But if we don't journey to the interior, of ourselves and our world, we will never emerge with the realization that we *do* have deep longings, that we *are* possibly designed for a different world, and that we *can* have hope that one day, these longings—the gentle whisperings of our heart—can be fulfilled.

In this book I want to explain this deep-down longing that I believe is in every one of us—a longing that can only be met with one thing, or rather one person. This isn't some short-lived, unfulfilling high that crumbles as soon as the dose wears off. I believe that the reason we have a longing for more is because we were *made* for more. We were made to know and be known by the one true God—to be in relationship with him. I believe that a life in relationship with God is the life you and I were made for.

2

On God

Who is God?

I don't know how you picture God, or if in fact you do. In conversations with my friends I often hear that they "believe in God", but when we talk about what this god is like it quickly becomes apparent that we have very different ideas of how to answer the question 'Who is God?' To many it doesn't matter that there are so many ideas about who God is—but as soon as you start to insist that there is one true God, people get their feathers ruffled.

I loved my grandmother Judith very much. She wasn't a perfect woman. She suffered from depression, was frustrated being born in an era when women were restricted to being at home, and she longed for a career of her own. But I loved her big home-cooked meals. I loved her enjoyment of playing the piano, even when her arthritis made it painful. I loved her love for reading and the way she would cut out articles or write down quotes that inspired her, and stick them all around her home. I loved the way she fiercely loved my grandfather. I loved her deep, unfailing love for the God of the Bible.

As you read that paragraph about my grandmother, you started to know a little about her. If you read some of the letters she sent me, your view of her would become more accurate. But if you had actually met her, formed a relationship with her and read a personal memoir she had written, revealing who she was, you would know her much more intimately. You might start to get upset if someone who didn't know her just shrugged their shoulders when you tried to share what she was like, and brushed it off with a "Well, that idea of Judith is fine for you, but I have a different idea of who she was". You may get even more upset if you knew that their idea of my grandmother was totally inaccurate.

How do we know?

Just as there was only one Grandma Judy, there is only one true God. Just as I can say I really knew my Grandma Judy, I can also say that I know the one true God. Like an athlete doing the hurdles, this is the first one you need to grapple with in your exploration of Christianity. I believe that I know God because I have a book that he himself has written to explain who he is. I know God because I've spent time reading the words he's written.

The best way to know God is through what he says about himself. Lately, I've been enjoying some shows and movies on the British royal family. I feel like I've grown in my knowledge of the royals, but I'm aware that these are creative works meant to entertain, written by someone other than the Queen herself. The amazing thing about the Bible, though, is that the words found there actually come from God. He has given us written words that tell us who he is—God's words about himself. He hasn't left us needing to make guesses about what he is like.

But how can the Bible be written by God when he didn't actually put fingers to keyboard, or pen to paper, or ink to parchment? Wouldn't it read more like a biography rather than an autobiography? Like men writing about God rather than God revealing himself in his own words?

It's true that God himself didn't write the Bible with his own physical hand. It was human hands (actually about 40 different people altogether) that literally wrote the Bible. But look at what Peter, one of the Bible's writers, said:

For prophecy never had its origin in the human will,
but prophets, though human, spoke from God as they
were carried along by the Holy Spirit. (2 Peter 1:21)

Basically, Peter argues that as a spokesperson for God, he didn't wake up one morning and think, "Hey, I'm going to pretend I'm God today and write a book to fool everyone". Instead, Peter explains, God inspired him by telling him what to write. The words of the Bible were *breathed out by God*— they came from the very mouth of God (2 Timothy 3:16).

It's because this book is written by God that it's absolutely trustworthy. When people tell us what they're like, we might wonder if they're telling us the full picture. No human being has perfect self-awareness or knowledge of every circumstance they're in. And sometimes people deliberately give false impressions—have you ever looked at a Facebook profile and thought "surely no-one's life can be *that* perfect?!"

But that's not the case with God. God *is* perfect. He never deceives, distorts or misrepresents. As the Bible says: "God is not human, that he should lie, not a human being, that he should change his mind" (Numbers 23:19). God is all-knowing, so there is not a single fact that he overlooked when he chose what words to give us in the Bible. He didn't decide to gloss over the moments when people he loved messed up, nor did he leave certain people out of the family tree because they made embarrassing mistakes. Unlike a human document, the Bible is *totally* trustworthy and contains all we need to know—his perfection juxtaposed against the messy history of the world.

We can and should trust God's words above everything else we think is true, simply because they are God's words. After all, "the words of the LORD are flawless" (Psalm 12:6).

Although it's a collection of 66 books written over 1500 years, because the Bible was written by God it amazingly tells one complete story. It tells the story of God and his desire to be in relationship with his people. It's a beautiful story; a story of love, a story of sacrifice, a story of adventure. It's a story that makes sense of God, the world and ourselves. It explains the life we were made for.

The road ahead

In this book I explain how we were made to know and be known by God. I believe God's words to be what they say they are, so that's why I use the Bible as the basis for everything I say here. Because God makes himself known in the Bible, it makes sense to use this as our foundation. Before you get anxious that you don't know enough about the Bible to read this book, please don't worry. We'll start together at the beginning of the Bible and work our way to the end, summarizing bits here and there and skipping over big chunks.

More than anything though, I encourage you to look at the Bible for yourself—the God of the universe's writing is so much better than mine! I'll include the Bible reference of the parts that I quote here so you can find them for yourself.

You may end this book with more questions than you started with, but my hope is that you will see God for who he is and bring your questions and longings to him, knowing that he offers you far more than anyone or anything else could.

3
A world without longing

Whenever Louis Armstrong's song 'What a Wonderful World' drifts onto the radio, I can't help but sing along. There's something in those simplistic but lilting lyrics that causes me to look up and out to the world around me. As Armstrong sings of seeing things like trees of green, red roses, skies of blue and clouds of white, he thinks to himself, "what a wonderful world".

In 2017 this song turned 50 years old. It may surprise you to know that Armstrong recorded this song at a tumultuous time in history that included the Vietnam War, the civil rights and feminist movements, and political upheaval across the globe. Amidst all this, Armstrong recorded a song about how he chose to see the beauty of the world around him.

It seems to be a daily process of *choosing* to look for beauty in our broken world, which is often so full of struggles, pain and suffering. Has it always been this way—a matter of choosing to find the good and overlooking the bad?

Recently, a friend's little daughter was asking her how the trees came to be, how the sky was made, how the flowers were born. My friend told her some of the many different things that people believe about how the world was created. As she explained the different ideas she'd presented to her daughter, I couldn't help but think, "So which belief is right? Which one will you and your daughter take hold of?" What is the real answer to the age-old question of how everything came to be?

The Bible gives a very clear answer to this question. The first thing it tells us about God is that he is our creator. In chapters 1 and 2 of the book of Genesis (the first book in the Bible) we learn that before there was anything, there was God. God is eternal—he had no beginning and has no end. And he created everything—from the highest mountain peak, to the deepest point of the sea floor, from the gigantic elephant to the tiny ladybird. All things were made by him. And he made all things simply by speaking. He spoke and creatures bounced, hopped and swam. They came to exist.

God created the whole universe, and he created human beings as the pinnacle of his creation. It was only after he had made people that God said his creation was "*very* good" (Genesis 1:31).[2] And because he created the world, he is the

---

2   As an aside, it's important to say that the account of creation in Genesis does not claim to be a *scientific* account of how the world was made. It definitely claims to be a true story (because it comes from God) but it isn't trying to give a scientific explanation of how the world was made. The important thing to take from Genesis is that God made the world. Without him, nothing would exist.

supreme ruler in charge of everyone and everything. But unlike human rulers who are capable of evil and corruption, the Bible tells us that God is also utterly *good* (Psalm 136). Because God is so good, he would always do what was best for his subjects.

The Bible paints the most beautiful picture of the world that God created for his people. Right back in the beginning, it wasn't a matter of only choosing to see the beauty; it was only beauty that existed. The world was new, it was untarnished and it was marvellous. The Bible tells of a garden named 'Eden', where God planted trees that were beautiful to look at and good for food. There was a glistening river system, flowing through the garden. There were wild animals and birds that dwelt alongside mankind. There was peace— glorious, sustaining, peace.

But this wasn't the most wonderful thing. The Bible tells us that in the garden, the man and woman (named Adam and Eve) had an intimate relationship with God. God walked with them in the cool of the day and spoke with them. In an overflow of his love, God had created these people and he delighted in spending time with them.

Recently my husband Dave and I took our three young children camping. As I watched Dave play with them on the beach, I thought about how we had these little people as a means of reflecting the love we shared. They look and act a little bit like a hybrid of Dave and me. We love spending time with them, listening to them, marvelling at them, chatting with them.

Now, take this idea, and magnify and perfect it. God created man and woman to reflect his image and likeness. As God's love burst forth, he created people to be in perfect, harmonious relationship with himself. In this relationship, there was no longing. God provided all that his people needed, physically, emotionally, mentally and spiritually. There was nothing that they found wanting. God's people lived in a truly wonderful world.

4
What went wrong?

The world today is far from this place of perfection. At worst we have war, abuse, murder, rape and shattered relationships. Even in our most secure relationships there is sometimes still hurt and angst and pain. And what about that deep-down niggle that there is more to life than this? Our world is a far cry from the garden of Eden. So what happened to this perfect world the Bible describes?

A choice between good and evil

In Genesis 2, we read that God placed "the tree of the knowledge of good and evil" (quite a name!) in his perfect world. God had given his people everything, with only one limitation: in a garden *full* of trees and *full* of fruit, they were not to eat from this one tree.

Adam and Eve had the freedom to choose what fruit they would eat, but they couldn't choose what the consequences were if they decided to eat from the forbidden tree. God created Adam and Eve to be perfectly innocent and pure, knowing only what was good. But if they ate from the tree, they would be taking on themselves the right to decide what was good and evil. They would be usurping God's authority as their loving ruler. And God told them that the result of this would be death. God warned them in stark terms that if they ate from this tree, they would die (Genesis 2:17).

Sometimes in fiction we read of this tree as being a bit like the poisonous apple in Snow White; that there was something inherent in it that would have brought death and destruction. But that isn't the case. God had created all things and all things were good. It was in the *choosing* to usurp God that death would come into their perfect world.

So God's people had to choose to be obedient, to trust that God knew best, to believe that what God said was good. After all, he had already been so generous to them! How could they rebel against such a loving God?

Choosing evil

As a mum to three young children, I sometimes find I am more surprised by obedience than disobedience. I certainly remember moments growing up when I chose to deliberately do the opposite of what my parents said, and often the consequences weren't good. Often they knew better than I did.

If we were to continue tracing every bad decision back through time, we would eventually get to the garden called

Eden, two people named Adam and Eve and a tree with fruit. In a tragic mistake that would have hideous consequences, Adam and Eve thought they knew better than God.

Adam and Eve had a little help making this very poor decision though. Genesis 3 tells us about an evil serpent weaselling his way into the garden. The serpent approaches Eve first and causes her to question God's words: "Did God *really* say, 'You must not eat from any tree in the garden'?" (Genesis 3:1). Eve points out that God actually said they couldn't eat from just *one* specific tree, or they would die. They could eat from any of the others.

But this slippery snake doesn't stop there. He lures Eve into further discussion and suggests that God had lied to them in his instruction, that he was actually keeping something from them. Surely they won't die if they taste the fruit from the forbidden tree. On the contrary, they will be *like* God because they will know good and evil.

As soon as Satan weaves his lie, Eve is hooked. She is no longer content with being a creature under a good and loving creator. She looks. She longs. She reaches. She eats. And she doesn't want to be on her own in the venture, so she shares the fruit with her husband. And just like that, evil had the victory. In one decision, death comes into play.

God's initial response

I love the self-help genre. Whether it's a guide to gardening, or a TV series on home improvements, or a DIY blog… I get excited looking at them. Pinterest boards filled with 'before and afters' make my heart race. Recently a 'how to' blog post on de-cluttering made me salivate a little. There's something satisfying about doing things for yourself. It makes me feel capable, productive and successful.

As a blogger, I notice fairly frequently the 'listicles' that come across my social media feeds. Why are '7 steps to…' and the like so popular? Well, it's because they deliver a promise. The headline cries out to us in the midst of our busyness that the time we invest in reading the article will deliver instant results—in just 7 steps!

If I was Eve, I'm sure I would be looking around for a blog post on '7 steps to un-eat the fruit'. Because the moment the fruit touched Eve's lips, she felt shame. We know this, because the Bible tells us that Adam and Eve knew they were naked and they went about trying to cover it up (Genesis 3:7). All of a sudden, Adam and Eve were no longer open about everything. They wanted to cover their bodies, to hide their vulnerability from each other. Their 'private parts' became private. They had lost their innocence.

The shame continues as God comes to walk in the garden of Eden in the cool of the day. Adam and Eve hide from God in their shame. Of course, this all-knowing God immediately knew what they had done, but they tried their hand at hiding anyway—just like little children.

Have you ever felt that cathartic release of adrenalin after having a good yell at someone or something? Whether it's letting out an expletive when you drop something on your foot, or having a yelling match with one of your loved ones, (especially if they're the ones who have wronged you)… it's just so satisfying.

If ever there was a moment where rage was justified, it would be at this point in history. God had given Adam and Eve everything—a truly perfect world. But they had done the one thing he asked them not to do. They had defied their generous God and turned their back on what he had said. Yet God came walking in the garden not to have a cathartic release of spewing anger, or laugh at the folly of the people he had created, which is so often the way people want to depict God. Rather, he came because of his loving mercy. You see, God called to his people, knowing that the answer to shame is forgiveness. He calls to them and gently asks them how they knew they were naked and why they hid from him. And he generously gives them clothes to cover their nakedness and shame.

God offers this undeserved favour to his people, but there were still consequences to their actions. After all, God had said there *would* be consequences if they ate from the tree and God is always true to his word. In their decision to eat the fruit, Adam and Eve had effectively told God to go away. They didn't want him to tell them what to do. And in response to their rebellion, that's exactly what God did. God withdrew from his people and cut them off from himself.

The Bible tells us again and again that one of God's attributes is that he is *holy*—that means he is perfectly pure, innocent and good. And a holy God can't have anything to do with evil because he's so pure. Evil simply can't exist in his presence. So now that Adam and Eve have rebelled against him, God banishes them from the garden. Adam and Eve, who had only that morning been in a perfect relationship with the God of the universe, have now been cast away from his presence.

And because they were now cut off from God who is the source of life, *death would now exist*. There would be a designated time period that they were allowed to live on the earth for and then they would be no more.

There was no DIY quick-fix here. There was just the reality of living a life separated from God, a life of regret and longing. Had they not rebelled, Adam and Eve would have lived *eternally* with God. But now they were separated from him. They had to live away from his presence and would one day die.

Life became hard because of what they had done—life was no longer as it was meant to be. They were made for life in a perfect world, in perfect relationship with their God and each other. And I'm sure that from the moment they'd taken their first bite, they had a deep-down longing for the life they were made for.

5
Making sense of our longing

The Bible calls this rebellion of Adam and Eve 'sin'. When Adam and Eve chose to eat the fruit, sin entered their veins and weaved its tentacles through their beings. Because sin was coursing through Adam and Eve's veins, it would pass on to their children and their children's children—even to us. Like Adam and Eve, we are also rebels or sinners.

You may feel like a pretty good person, and on the whole I think a lot of people on earth seem like fairly decent people. You may love others, you may care for the sick and downtrodden, you may work hard, you might even take that extra change back to the checkout if they give you too much. So this whole thing of you and me being sinners doesn't sit well with you. Surely sinners are murderers and people like that, people who do really terrible things—not ordinary people like you and me.

But the Bible defines sin differently. It says that every single person (apart from one) who has ever walked the earth is a sinner. Sin isn't a specific action. It's an attitude of the heart that de-thrones God and puts ourselves centre-stage.

Take a glance at your current relationships and you might see how this is true. When I look at myself I realize that I fight with my husband because I want to be right; I get angry at my kids because they aren't letting me have 'mummy time'; I get jealous of my friend because she has a bigger house, dresses immaculately and drives the car *I* want to be driving. We're conditioned not to think about these kinds of things as 'sin'. But this is exactly what the Bible says it is—putting ourselves at the centre, putting *our* needs first, setting ourselves up as the rulers of our lives, thinking *we* know best and turning our backs on God—the only true king, who is deserving of our greatest love, attention and obedience.

Just like the oxygen that fills our lungs in order for us to live, sin is part of our humanity. Instead of living in submission to a holy God, we make decisions every single day that reinforce the fact that we want to be the god of our life. We reject the one true God over and over again—the one who made us and gives us life every day. We want what *we* want and we want it now. *Just* like Adam and Eve.

Do you see that attitude in yourself?

Living with a sense of longing

We think we're benefiting ourselves by putting ourselves at the centre and making *our* needs the top priority. But in a great twist of irony, we are doing the very opposite. For one thing, we were *made* for relationship with God. So by constantly pursuing our own selfish desires rather than God himself, we're going against the very way we've been designed to function.

I truly believe that this explains that deep-down inkling that there's more to life than this. Deep down we crave what we were made for—that which has been taken away because of our rebellion.

But just as our sin has taken away the only thing that would truly satisfy us, it's also our sin that stops us reaching out to God and living the life we were made for. Just like Adam and Eve, we continue to think that life would be better without God, when in reality a personal relationship with God is the one thing we really need.

So instead we foolishly try with all our might to satisfy that deep-down longing with other things—I go on a shopping spree hoping the joy of a new purchase will dim my need; I seek people's affirmation in the hope it will help me feel better about myself; I spend ages applying makeup in the hope that the mask will overcome the depth of my insecurities and my need to feel loved, valued, accepted.

But that longing will never be fulfilled by anything other than a relationship with the God who made us. Just as a square peg cannot fill a round hole, neither can the 'God-shaped chasm' inside each of us be filled by anyone or anything other than God. This constant desire to fill our God-chasm with other things is a never-ending cycle of disappointment and unmet fulfilment. And it's all because of sin.

Judgement from God

Sin makes sense of our restlessness and longing for more. But there's a more serious and eternal consequence to our sin. God cares that we don't treat him as he deserves and, just like Adam and Eve, we stand guilty before the God of the universe. Just as he did with Adam and Eve, God passes a sentence on us for our disobedience, for the way we have sought to live independently from our creator. In the Bible we are told that because of our sin "people are destined to die once, and after that to face judgement" (Hebrews 9:27). If we are found guilty under God's judgement, then we face being cut off from God's presence forever.

God hates all sin because it's completely opposed to his character. As one of the Bible's prophets says to God, "Your eyes are too pure to look on evil; you cannot tolerate wrongdoing" (Habakkuk 1:13). And if God just said, "Forget about your rebellion, it doesn't really matter", what kind of God would we have? God is not one of those pushover parents who looks indulgently on their child as they treat them and others like dirt. He is loving, but his love is not weakly sentimental.

Maybe you think God could or should just overlook your sin—because after all, it's not that bad compared to others. Surely God's judgement should be reserved for the people who have done really bad things—the child molesters, the rapists, the murderers of this world. We want God's judgement for *those* sinners, for the real evil in our world, but not for us.

There is some wickedness in the world that we can easily recognize—things like murder, sexual assault, violence. Evil acts that we fear. My heart aches for you if you have experienced such evil. But if we compare our sin to these things then we've failed to understand the nature of our rejection of God. Whether we reject God by lying or cheating or by killing someone, the rejection is the same because the motivation behind it is the same. In all of this we're telling God we don't want him, we don't want to follow his ways. Like Adam and Eve, we want God's world without God.

God cares enough about humanity to take our rebellion seriously. He doesn't change the rules for anyone, anywhere, for any reason. You can be certain that he'll act consistently with his character—because he is holy, he loves goodness and hates evil. It's because of this that you can know exactly where you stand with him. God is a fair judge who needs to punish sin.

We're all guilty before God. What's more, we can't just stop being sinful. Sin is in our veins. Remember, it's like the oxygen we breathe. We can't get away from it. And while we're sinful, we're still guilty before God. While we're sinful, it's very hard to truly seek God—the voice in our head is still whispering "self, self, self". So is there a way out of this predicament?

6
God's plan

God is the ultimate planner. A common misconception is that God planned this wonderful world and then he was caught unawares when Adam and Eve messed up his plan. This couldn't be further from the truth.

One of the amazing things about God is that he is all-knowing. He knew that Adam and Eve would make the wrong decision and reject him and his loving rule of their lives, yet he chose to make them anyway. He knew you and I would mess up too.

For me, even despite my best efforts, things often don't go to plan. I host a dinner party to have fun with friends but my timing is off with the cooking so I get stressed and I can't enjoy the night. I go out for a relaxing coffee with a friend and end up getting upset by some throwaway comment she makes. I go on a beachside holiday but it rains the whole time.

But God's plan is 100 per cent spot on *all the time*. So once Adam and Eve sinned, his plan continued. He didn't come up with a Plan B; Plan A was still in action. Although sin had entered the world and people were now cut off from the life they were made for, God had a plan to save his people.

A promised king

Long ago God promised his people that he would send a rescuer to restore the broken relationship between God and humanity. The whole Old Testament section of the Bible talks about God's promise to send a king to rescue his people. The prophet Isaiah said this king would be called "Wonderful Counsellor", "Mighty God", "Everlasting Father", "Prince of Peace", and would possess an everlasting kingdom (Isaiah 9:6-7).

God is justified in his anger and judgement of human rebellion. But in his amazing love and kindness, God chose to intervene in our predicament and provided a way out. He didn't have to, but out of love and mercy for his people, God did something to break the cycle of sin and death, and to make it possible for us to return to him.

God had always promised to send a rescuer, and over 2000 years ago, the promise came true, and the rescuer came to earth. But this long-promised king arrived in quite an unexpected way…

Jesus: God as a baby

Have you ever been to a school nativity play? If you have, then you're probably familiar with the set-up: angels and shepherds, Mary, Joseph and the innkeeper, and the cute little baby all wrapped up in a manger.

But just pause for a moment. Don't let any familiarity with the story cause you to look past just how strange this all is. Even in the first century, when Jesus' birth took place, this was a very unusual scenario.

In the Gospel of Luke, the story begins with an angel taking a message to a teenage girl, a message that would tilt her world on its axis and change the course of history. Understandably, this girl, Mary, is a bit shocked—she sees an angel standing in front of her saying she is favoured and that God is with her. The angel tells Mary that she'll conceive a baby and will bear God's Son, and name him Jesus:

> "Do not be afraid, Mary; you have found favour with God. You will conceive and give birth to a son, and you are to call him Jesus. He will be great and will be called the Son of the Most High. The Lord God will give him the throne of his father David, and he will reign over Jacob's descendants forever; his kingdom will never end." (Luke 1:30-33)

This is quite an announcement. Mary is a virgin so naturally she wonders how she will conceive a child. The angel goes on to explain that the Holy Spirit will intervene and be with her—essentially the baby will grow as an act of God. Although this baby will be born of a woman, he is 'conceived' by God. This is fitting, really, because the angel also says that this human baby will be the Son of the Most High God. He will be both fully God and fully human. *This* was the king God had promised to send as a rescuer.

Imagine that for a start to motherhood—an angel letting you know you are going to have a baby who is put there in your womb by God, and finding out that this baby will be the very Son of God. As a Jew, Mary would have been familiar with the promises God had made thousands of years earlier to send an eternal king to rescue his people. But to find out that *she* was going to carry this king must have been a total shock, to say the least! But God, in his mercy, goes ahead of Mary and tells her "do not be afraid". He has also grown in her a heart of trust, so that she responds with the beautiful words: "I am the Lord's servant… May your word to me be fulfilled" (Luke 1:38).

I remember those months leading up to the birth of my first child. I was filled with awe at this little person growing inside me and fear and trepidation too—I was completely unsure how I would do the whole mothering thing. I did everything I could to prepare. I read parenting books, I attended prenatal classes, I wrote out a birth plan. I even remember sitting down with my husband, mother (a midwife) and sister (a trainee-midwife) who formed my birthing team, in order to explain to them how I wanted my labour to go.

No such plans were possible for Mary. As the time came for her baby to be born, a census was decreed. Unlike modern censuses, which can be carried out online or by post, first-century censuses required all people to return to their hometown and register. So Joseph had to return to his hometown of Bethlehem, taking his pregnant fiancée Mary with him. This was before Booking.com, and because the town was now so busy, there was nowhere for them to stay. Everywhere had 'no vacancy' signs. So Joseph and Mary were forced to take refuge in a room that was meant for animals.[3] Can you imagine how the pregnant, teenage Mary would have felt?

The Bible tells us that it's in this humble place that Mary gives birth to Jesus, and she lays him in a manger to sleep. Our modern-day nativities present this as quite a cosy little scene. But that is *far* from the first-century reality. In reality it would have been quite an unsanitary and unpleasant environment for a child to be born.

But remember, this was not just any child. The angel told Mary that this baby Jesus was the Son of the Most High God—a king, whose kingdom would never end. And here is the Son of God, being born as a tiny, fragile human baby, to a humble teenage girl, in a nasty, smelly place and sleeping in an animal feeding trough.

To give some perspective, when the Duchess of Cambridge gave birth to her royal babies, she had a 23-person medical team that was permanently on call for *three* months prior to their births. The royal babies were born in a private maternity unit in the grounds of St Mary's Hospital in London that comes complete with art installations, chef-made food and the option of ordering champagne to toast the baby's arrival. Now *that* is what we'd expect for a royal birth.[4]

---

3   Despite the popular depictions of nativity scenes, the Bible doesn't actually tell us that Jesus was born in a stable. The idea of a stable comes partly from mention of Jesus being placed in a manger (Luke 2:7), which of course suggests animals were present... and we assume animals are usually kept in a stable! But in first-century Palestine, animals were often kept in a space at the bottom of the house at night. So it's very possible that Jesus was actually born in a house rather than a stable.

4   Rebecca English, 'Call *all* the midwives!', *The Daily Mail Australia*, 25 May 2016 (viewed 21 December 2017): www.dailymail.co.uk/news/article-3607884/Call-midwives-Kate-23-strong-medical-team-George-Charlotte-s-births.html

Surely the Son of God could have chosen an arrival a million times more lovely or impressive than the private wing of St Mary's Hospital. But the God who made the whole universe just by speaking now saw fit to come to earth in the most vulnerable way—as a little baby born into hardship and humility.

So this really begs the question: why? Why would God choose a humble birth over a private suite and send his magnificent Son to earth in such a way?

Well, this king's humble arrival reveals *much* about what he had come to earth to do. This example of humility and hardship is something that would characterize Jesus' life as he grew into adulthood.

Although Jesus was in his very nature God, and deserved all the honour and privilege and glory that God deserves, he was willing to lay all this aside. And he did it for the sake of his people—people like you and me who were riddled with sin and a longing for more. Jesus chose to humble himself and endure hardship all through his life so that he might overcome our predicament. God's Son arrived into the mess of this world because he had come to rescue those who lived amongst the mess. He humbled himself for our sake, to bring us back into relationship with the God each of us have sinfully rejected.

7

Jesus the Son

Just as Jesus came into the world in poverty and hardship, so his life continued that way. He didn't live in a remote paradise somewhere; he grew up experiencing the everyday realities of human life. He lived the real life of a real man. He was a child, then he was a teenager, and he learned the carpentry trade from his father, Joseph.

At the age of 30, though, Jesus began something that was far from ordinary—what we now call his 'public ministry'. He left his home and his family and started carrying out the special work that God had planned for him to do.

His ministry begins with a pretty special event. Jesus is baptized by his cousin John in the Jordan River, at which point God's voice sounds from heaven, declaring "This is my Son, whom I love; with him I am well pleased" (Matthew 3:17). How's that for affirmation? God the Father says that

Jesus is his beloved Son and that he's pleased with him.

This gives us an insight into the uniqueness of Jesus' life so far. Although Jesus knew the sometimes hard realities of everyday life, his life was also marked by perfect love, devotion and obedience to God as his Father. Even when he went through those teenage years, in every aspect of his life, he listened and obeyed God. Now at 30, just before his ministry gets into full-gear, God says to Jesus that he was *pleased* with him. No other human who has ever walked the earth has perfectly obeyed God. God had not been fully pleased with any other person—except Jesus. And we get a clear picture of Jesus' perfect obedience in the extraordinary events that come after his baptism.

Given the astounding affirmation that God has made about Jesus, what follows next is a bit of a surprise. God leads Jesus into the wilderness. It was a barren, hostile and remote place in the Judean desert. For most of us, when our parents tell us they're proud of us, it's often followed by a reward. Or at least, it certainly isn't followed by what seems like punishment. But now, God leads his beloved Son Jesus to a horrible wilderness. And Jesus willingly goes. He goes there for a reason—to be tempted by the devil.

One of my current battles is with a night-time chocolate craving. As soon as it hits 8pm, my belly starts to rumble. I've tried replacing the chocolate with almonds, and I've tried just leaving chocolate out of the trolley when I go grocery shopping. But somehow, I still manage to find a bag of peanut M&Ms in my pantry that are calling my name when I'm tired. My willpower just isn't enough to fight the battle.

It's this kind of thing that we're prone to think of as 'temptation'. But for Jesus, his temptation wasn't just about petty chocolate and a little bit of tiredness. It was much, much more significant.

Jesus went into this desolate, hostile place, and went without food for 40 days and 40 nights. He was starving. By the end of this time, he would have been emaciated, gaunt and weak. And that slippery serpent Satan from back in the garden decides this is the perfect opportunity to launch another attack on God's good plan.

His strategy is the same as it was with Adam and Eve. Satan wants Jesus to question whether what God said was really true, if God really had his best interests at heart. When Jesus is at his very weakest, Satan says "*If* you are the Son of God, tell these stones to become bread" (Matthew 4:3).

God has already declared to Jesus that he is his beloved Son. But Satan wants Jesus to think that if he were really the Son of God, surely things would be going a little better. Jesus is in a wretched, miserable place forsaken by everybody. The question behind the question is "Does your Father really care for you, Jesus? Is he really doing what's best for you? Shouldn't you just take matters into your own hands here, and give yourself some bread?"

Satan desperately wants Jesus to distrust God's plan for him. But where Adam and Eve failed and gave in to Satan's temptation, Jesus triumphs. Jesus had all the power of God; he so easily could have made the stones turn into bread. But instead he answers by quoting an earlier part of the Bible— he answers the devil's words with God's words! "Man shall not live on bread alone, but on every word that comes from the mouth of God" (Matthew 4:4). Jesus shows that he trusts God's promise to care for him. He is dependent on God who alone is the giver and sustainer of life. He won't do what

Satan says. He trusts *God's* words to be true.

When Satan tempted Adam and Eve back in the garden of Eden, they were surrounded by so many other options for food. They were living in the most beautiful garden you could imagine and they walked with God. All they had to do was pick another piece of fruit off a different tree that day to please God. For Jesus, the opposite was true. He had no other source of food, he was starving, but *still* he trusts God's words to be true and is obedient to his Father.

Two more times Satan tempts Jesus to choose evil over God. He suggests to Jesus that he should enter into partnership with him and avoid the path of suffering and hardship. Then he tempts Jesus to create a definite proof of his Father's care by doing something God had not asked him to do. Both times Jesus turns again to God's words to rebut the lies of Satan. Eventually, realizing that victory would not be his, the devil left Jesus and angels attended him, marking the end of Jesus' time in the wilderness (Matthew 4:5-11).

The Bible says that Jesus was "tempted in every way, just as we are—yet he did not sin" (Hebrews 4:15). Indeed, he is the only human being to have *never* sinned. Unlike Adam and Eve, unlike you and me, he chose humility over pride, and prioritized relationship with God over selfish gain, time after time. God was right to be pleased with his perfect Son. Jesus was the only person who lived life as it was meant to be lived, in perfect submission to God's will. Yet in an amazing and unexpected way, it would be through Jesus' perfect obedience that God would deal with our *dis*obedience and enable us to live the life we were made for.

8

Jesus the Life-Giver

Jesus was not only extraordinary in his loving obedience to his Father, but also in the love he showed other people. Many of us try to distance ourselves from the 'unsavoury' characters in our lives, but Jesus—who was totally perfect and had more reason than anyone to remove himself from sinful people—did the exact opposite. He came alongside sinful, needy and vulnerable people and associated with the downtrodden. And he offered them true hope and meaning in the face of their greatest longings. He showed them that it's only *he* who could answer their yearnings for more. As I read of Jesus' interactions with people in the Bible, I can't help but be amazed at the way Jesus loves and cares for them, while making these extraordinary claims. Let's read some of these accounts now.

Jesus and a bleeding woman (Luke 8:43-48)

Growing up in a family of three girls, with a mother who was a nurse and midwife, and a younger sister who went on to follow in my mum's footsteps, there was always a degree of open discussion about birth, breastfeeding and a woman's monthly cycle. Nevertheless I still remember the horror with which my 13-year-old self watched a sex education video in science class about a young girl beginning her monthly period. In what was possibly the most awkward scenario I could imagine, when this girl got her first period her father took her to get a chocolate éclair to 'celebrate' her officially 'becoming a woman'. I was horrified. And I was filled with terror at the thought of my dad wanting to do something similar when my time came. Despite my family's openness, there was still a stigma in my 13-year-old mind around the oh-so-pretty topic of menstrual bleeding.

Perhaps for these reasons, I've always felt for a woman in the Bible who has become known simply as 'the bleeding woman'. She was a woman whose monthly discharge never stopped. There was no cycle for her—her bleeding had continued non-stop for 12 years. I can't even imagine it.

The Bible tells us that no-one could heal this woman. She'd spent all her money visiting doctor after doctor. But instead of getting better, she had actually grown worse.

Her condition wasn't just unpleasant, or even just painful. It had major social and cultural implications. This woman was a Jew and so culturally her bleeding would have meant she was considered 'unclean'. According to Jewish law, everything she touched—every article of clothing, every seat, every implement—also became unclean and had to be washed before others touched or used it. Likewise, every *person* who did so much as even brush up against her would also become unclean.

Just imagine this woman's isolation. Her life would have been that of continual broken relationship. She would have been an outcast simply because of the hassle it was to visit her. If someone popped in for a cup of tea, they would have had to undertake ceremonial washing afterwards. If she attended a wedding, unless she washed everything she touched, she would have knowingly been making others unclean. After a time, she would have simply been left off the guest list to events and would have been confined to her home. The frustration and desperation of this woman, now poverty-stricken, would have been immense. She was alone and hopeless; longing for relationship but unable to practically attain it.

Into this woman's life enters Jesus. She's heard whispers about this man who had been healing people from their sicknesses. And on this day, he is passing through her village. She is overcome with sheer desperation. Although it was going to mean making others unclean, she decides she must approach Jesus. She believes Jesus is her only chance—that if she could simply touch the hem of his clothes, he could heal her. So, hoping to go unnoticed, she crawls into the jostling crowd and she manages to reach out to the fringe of Jesus' cloak.

The moment she touches his cloak, this woman is healed. She feels the blood flow dry up. And she knows that it was Jesus who healed her. Jesus is so full of power that this simple act of touching his cloak has changed the trajectory of this woman's life forever!

Immediately Jesus asks, "Who touched me?" Jesus' followers point out that because there are so many people in the crowd around them, it could have been anyone (Luke 8:45). But Jesus knows that power has gone out from him. The woman, seeing that she could not go unnoticed any longer, comes trembling and falls at his feet. In the presence of all the people, she explained why she had touched him and how she had been instantly healed.

Jesus speaks to her tenderly and says, "Daughter, your faith has healed you. Go in peace" (Luke 8:48).

What astounding power, care and compassion Jesus shows her. His power is so great that a mere touch of his cloak is enough to do what years of medical treatment could not. This woman comes before him scared and trembling, unsure of the consequences of her actions, but he speaks to her with love and compassion, and offers her peace.

Here is a woman who brought her acute need and longing to Jesus in sheer desperation. And in his response, Jesus shows that those who are willing to come to him will be met with a warm and gracious response. He does what no-one else could do. She didn't do anything to deserve healing, but Jesus generously provided it anyway.

Jesus, a woman and a well (John 4:1-42)

One of my favourite stories in the Bible is found in John chapter 4, which tells us about Jesus' meeting with a Samaritan woman at a well. Here is another woman for whom life has been difficult. This woman was born with the wrong nationality—she was a Samaritan, and Jews despised Samaritans. She was a second-class citizen. On top of this she had a string of failed marriages and was living with a man who wasn't her husband. This was a serious issue in the first century. It meant that even in her own community she was shunned as an outcast. She had been labelled as 'used goods'. She was ostracized and marked as immoral.

In the days before plumbing, the Samaritan women walked to the well early in the morning, while it was still cool, to collect water for the day. But because this woman wasn't welcome in their company, she had to collect her water alone, in the heat of the middle of the day. Just imagine how hard this task would have been in the Middle Eastern heat. It was undoubtedly made harder by the fact that she was lonely and had no-one to share the burden with. I wonder sometimes whether this woman would have felt she deserved this hardship, whether she thought of it as a form of penance for her 'messed up life'.

Day after day this woman endured physical and social hardship as she went to collect water. But one day, something very surprising happened. There was a man at the well—not just any man, a Jewish man. And even more shockingly, he starts speaking to her. "Will you give me a drink?" he asks (John 4:7).

"You are a Jew and I am a Samaritan woman. How can you ask me for a drink?" the woman replies (John 4:9).

She hasn't yet worked out who Jesus is. But Jesus already knows everything about her. With amazing insight that could only come from God, he shows her that she is already known by him. "The fact is", Jesus says, "you have had five husbands and the man you now have is not your husband" (John 4:18).

Jesus knew her sinful situation. I'm sure this woman expected only more judgement and condemnation. But with radical love and compassion, Jesus invites her into conversation and shows her she is not beyond hope. He offers this woman what he calls 'living water'.

> "Everyone who drinks this water [physical water from a well] will be thirsty again, but whoever drinks the water I give them will *never* thirst. Indeed, the water I give them will become in them a spring of water welling up to eternal life." (John 4:13-14)

When we drink water, our thirst is satisfied for a while, yet we inevitably become thirsty again. But Jesus wanted this woman to see that he offers something that will satisfy her forever—an eternal relationship with God.

Everything else in life fades after a while. In this woman's case, she has tried to satisfy her longings with a series of relationships. Others of us fill it by seeking out amazing photos for Facebook, or by healthy eating, or by building up x amount of savings, or by getting kudos for brilliant children… the list goes on. These things usually feel good for a moment or two, but then we are looking for the next thing to fill our deepest longing. The initial spark of a relationship, the joy of a few kilos lost, a new purchase—it all feels good for a moment, but then we realize we are looking for more.

Jesus wants the woman to lift her eyes to see that he offers something of the greatest possible value, something that will never fade, and something no-one or nothing else can offer. He offers this same gift to us if we look to him.

This Samaritan woman was so amazed by her encounter with Jesus. He knew the skeletons in her closet, yet offered her salvation and eternal hope. When no-one else could see anything of value in this woman, he offered her a relationship with the God of the universe.

This woman can't help but go and speak about Jesus. She leaves her water jar at the well, and goes back to the town (where only that morning she was too intimated to go) and invites others to come and meet Jesus: "Come, see a man who told me everything I ever did. Could this be the Messiah?" (John 4:29).

Sometimes, I wonder whether women I meet are anything like the Samaritan woman. We get so good at putting up a facade, that often we don't reveal the 'real' us to anyone else. No-one even gets a glimpse of our skeletons that we keep hidden away. Jesus shows that no matter how chequered our past, or how much we've tried to satisfy our longings with the wrong things, we are not beyond the care and mercy of God. Jesus knew all about this woman and still offered to meet her deep-down thirst for hope, meaning and relationship.

Jesus shows he's the one to come to with our needs and longings and deep-down sense that there must be more. He even shows that he is the one who can give us an eternal relationship with the God who made us. But how does he actually go about making that possible? How does he make it possible for us to live the life we were made for?

9

Jesus the Saviour

Have you ever lost a loved one? Or even watched a loved one die? In my life, I have met a number of women feeling the full brute force of grief. Whether they've lost a husband, a child or a close friend, each one of them has experienced grief differently. It's personal and raw, sometimes coming in waves so intense, and at other times settling as a weight on their chest. When grief hits, we also question why it happened and more particularly, why it happened to us. We wonder whether any of our decisions could have led to a different outcome, whether there was anything we could have controlled to prevent the tragedy happening.

In Matthew 27:61 we read of a woman called Mary. For Mary, it had been a traumatic couple of days. One of her dearest friends had been arrested, publically ridiculed, and put before a corrupt judge and jury. But instead of receiving a mistrial, he had been wrongly convicted. Horrifically, Mary's friend had received the death penalty—he was brutally murdered in a public execution, with his body displayed for all to hurl insults at as they walked past his dead carcass. It all reeked of the most atrocious evil. And now she sat watching his body be buried in a tomb. On some level, her grief was probably only just beginning.

What made this tragedy even worse was that Mary's friend had been one of those likeable characters—he cared for the downtrodden, he took time to really listen, he had strength with grace, he spent time bouncing the village kids on his knee. Some scoffed at the company he kept, but it actually showed that he wasn't power-hungry, or proud. He was extremely intelligent and was able to reason with people. He was charismatic and drew people to himself to simply chat. But in it all he was humble. This was the problem.

The story of Mary's friend may sound a bit familiar to you, because strangely, Christians celebrate it each Easter. Mary's friend was Jesus.

Although Jesus was truly innocent, his claims had ruffled some feathers. Jesus had talked openly about the fact he was God's Son. He hung out with sinners and outcasts, and challenged the hypocritical attitudes and actions of the power-hungry religious leaders of his day. He was a threat to their authority, so they plotted to have him killed—and they succeeded. Jesus was crucified alongside two criminals.

This was a torturous method of execution in the ancient Roman world. Jesus was whipped, tortured and mocked before being nailed to a large wooden cross by his hands and feet, and left to hang for hours until death eventually came from exhaustion and an inability to breathe any longer.[5] His pain would have been immense. The boy who was born in a manger had grown up only to die on a cruel cross.

I can't imagine how Mary felt as she watched her innocent friend die in such pain. In addition to the mind-numbing grief and pain, she must also have been so confused. She thought that Jesus was the king that God had promised long ago who would come to save his people. Yet here he was dying the death of a thug. Surely, for someone so powerful something could and should have been done? But Jesus used his power to hold himself to the cross.

Why did Jesus die?

One thing is clear: Jesus didn't deserve to die. Unlike Adam and Eve, unlike you and me, Jesus didn't ever rebel against God, and he was the only person who perfectly loved other people. If death is the result of sin, then why did this sinless man die such a cruel and painful death? This is a hard thing for us to wrap our minds around.

Jesus' death was a crucial part of God's loving plan to intervene in our predicament and save us from ourselves.

---

5   There's been debate over the years as to how exactly crucifixion killed its victims. For example, an article in the Journal of the Royal Society of Medicine gave 9 different hypotheses about Jesus' precise cause of death, including asphyxiation, heart failure, a blood clot in the lungs, and hypovolemic shock, in which severe blood and fluid loss prevent the heart from pumping enough blood to the body, causing organ failure. But at a most basic level, crucifixion was designed to interfere with the prisoner's ability to breathe. See Patrick J Kiger, 'How did crucifixion kill a person?', *National Geographic*, 17 February 2017 (viewed 7 December 2017): www.channel.nationalgeographic.com/killing-jesus/articles/how-did-crucifixion-kill-a-person/

We are the guilty ones. *We* are the ones who deserved to be punished. For God to be fair and just, he was always going to have to punish our sin, just as he promised he would way back in the garden of Eden.

But here is the utterly astounding thing—Jesus chose to die in our place, to take the punishment we deserve. He took the entire force of God's judgement on himself, so that forgiveness might be possible for rebels like you and me.

This is huge. I know how cranky I can get when I see a bad driver on the road. If there was a police officer nearby, I'd certainly be drawing their attention to this lunatic behind the wheel—they made the mistake of driving dangerously; they deserve the consequences. But Jesus once again shows the ways of God are above our ways; he *chose* to take the punishment that we deserve, so that we didn't have to. Jesus had lived a perfect life and so was in a position to do that. He had no sins of his own, and so no punishment was due to him. So although he was without sin, he willingly accepted being forsaken by God and endured horrific evil.

Have a look at what the Gospel of Matthew says actually happened as Jesus died on the cross:

> From noon until three in the afternoon darkness came over all the land. About three in the afternoon Jesus cried out in a loud voice "*Eli, Eli, lema sabachthani?*" (which means "My God, my God, why have you forsaken me?").
>
> …
>
> At that moment the curtain of the temple was torn in two from top to bottom. (Matthew 27:45, 51)

This description seems a little random at first. These seem like quite odd details to include. What's the deal with a curtain being torn? But these details reveal a lot about what it meant for Jesus to die in our place.

As Jesus died on the cross he cried out, "My God, my God, why have you forsaken me?" Here, Jesus is declaring to the world, to you and me today, that he was forsaken by God. God turned his back on his Son so that you and I could be brought back into relationship with him. While God's heart was completely broken, his Son was too. The only person who never deserved to be separated from God, who knew what complete relationship with God felt like, was now rejected and alone.

We see the significance of this completely mind-boggling truth in the description of what happens to the temple curtain, which is torn in two. To give you a bit of background, the Jews had an elaborate system of worship that was conducted in the temple at Jerusalem. Certain parts of the temple were open to everyone, while other parts were open only to male Jews. In the centre of the temple was a place called the Holy of Holies, and only one person was ever allowed in there on one day in the entire year. This man was the High Priest, chosen from the Jews, chosen from the smaller tribe of Levi from within the Jewish nation. Can you see how restricted it was?

The Holy of Holies symbolized the presence of God with his people. It was a reminder to all who came to the temple that God is holy and mankind is sinful. It was also a reminder that God wanted to be with his people, to be accessible. But it was a clear statement that *sinful people cannot approach a holy God*.

So do you see the significance of the Bible telling us that when Jesus hung on the cross dying, the temple curtain that separated this holy place from the rest of the temple tore in two? When Jesus died his sin-bearing death on the cross, *he opened up a way of access into God's presence for anyone.* He opened up a way for sinful people to be in relationship with a holy God.

As the apostle Peter puts it: "Christ also suffered once for sins, the righteous for the unrighteous, to bring you to God" (1 Peter 3:18). What an astounding truth. Don't skip over it! Let it sink in, allowing the full weight of that statement to resonate. The perfect Son of God suffered and died for sinful and broken people like you and me for one purpose—to bring people like you and me to God.

As Jesus bore the burden for our sin he broke down the barrier between people and God that had come into existence because of sin. He endured a terrible punishment, so that we wouldn't have to. He opened the way back to God so that we might have a restored relationship with the God who made us.

Those watching Jesus die said that if Jesus was really God's Son, surely he could have saved himself. Jesus was certainly more than able to take himself off the cross if he had wanted. This is the man who healed the sick, restored sight to the blind and did all kinds of other astounding miracles. Yet he chose to stay there, to endure the cross. And he did it out of love for his people.

Thousands of years before Jesus came, the prophet Isaiah spoke about the way this promised king would save his people:

> But he was pierced for our transgressions,
>   he was crushed for our iniquities;
> the punishment that brought us peace was on him,
>   and by his wounds we are healed.

We all, like sheep, have gone astray,
  each of us has turned to our own way;
and the LORD has laid on him
  the iniquity of us all. (Isaiah 53:5-6)

The words 'iniquity' and 'transgression' essentially mean our sin. So it was for *our* sin that the Saviour would be pierced, crushed, wounded. And by these wounds, we can be healed—saved from the great separation between us and God. As Isaiah says, we have peace with God only through the punishment that was laid on Jesus.

This peace with God is an undeserved gift. We didn't do anything to deserve it. We never could have earned it. This what the Bible calls grace.

In a series of very candid interviews U2 front man Bono says the thing that marks out Christianity from other religions is the difference between karma and grace.[6] The world operates on karma—what goes around comes around, be nice to others and they will be nice to you, basically be good so that good things will happen to you. It's a self-interested morality. But Bono points out how God's grace turns karma on its head. And he is exactly right. While we are swimming in the mucky water of sin, God saves us and takes us to drink deeply from fresh and living water. He lifts us out of that cesspool of selfishness, even though we don't deserve anything but judgement and death. It's all because of him offering us grace—what we don't deserve. It's a gift, not a reward.

---

6 *Bono: In Conversation with Michka Assayas*, Riverhead Books, New York, 2006, p. 204.

But because of his great love for us, God, who is rich in mercy, made us alive with Christ even when we were dead in transgressions—it is by grace you have been saved. (Ephesians 2:4)

Death was not the end

Mary didn't understand any of this as she watched Jesus die. Far from seeing it as a victory over sin, to her it looked like Satan had won and Jesus had lost. But in time she'd come to see that the victory really did belong to Jesus.

Three days after Jesus died and was buried, the Bible tells us that Mary along with two other women were on their way to grieve by the tomb where Jesus' body had been laid. They were hoping to rub special embalming spices on his body, although they weren't entirely sure how they would get past the huge stone that had been rolled across the entrance, and into the tomb (Mark 16:1-3).

But when the women arrived at the tomb, they saw their worry had been in vain. The stone had already been rolled away. This is what the Gospel of Mark says happened next:

As they entered the tomb, they saw a young man dressed in a white robe sitting on the right side, and they were alarmed.

"Don't be alarmed," he said. "You are looking for Jesus the Nazarene, who was crucified. He has risen! He is not here. See the place where they laid him." (Mark 16:5-6)

Can you imagine what these women were thinking and feeling? What an incredible claim this man was making. But could it possibly be true? Could their dear friend Jesus really be alive?

The Bible says the risen Jesus appeared to Mary, and asks her why she's crying. When he calls her lovingly by name, she knows straight away that it's Jesus (John 20:15-16). Can you imagine the joy that would have replaced her overwhelming grief? The hope and excitement that replaced her despair? Often there is nothing a grieving person wants more than to see their loved one again in the flesh. And here Jesus was, in the flesh! Jesus then appeared to his other followers (John 20:19-20). The Gospel of Luke tells us that Jesus even invited the disciples to touch him to confirm that it was really him, and not some kind of ghost (Luke 24:37-43). Around 20 years after the event, the apostle Paul gives a list of all the eyewitnesses who saw the risen Jesus, which includes more than 500 people (1 Corinthians 15:5-8).

Those who saw the risen Jesus were transformed from weak and cowardly men into bold and courageous witnesses. At the time of Jesus' arrest they all took the cowardly route, leaving their friend Jesus to the torture and torment, fearfully fleeing to preserve their own lives (Mark 14:50). But somehow, within a matter of months they were willing to stand in front of the Council that had condemned Jesus and to boldly preach about him. Why the dramatic change? It was the total certainty that Jesus really had risen from the dead, that he was alive and was God's promised king (Acts 4:10).

This might seem like a hard thing to believe. But if Jesus really was the Son of God then it actually makes sense that God would raise him from the dead. It's true that in our experience no-one has risen from the dead. But in our experience, we have also never seen God in the flesh! If God's Son really came to earth and dwelled in human flesh, isn't it perfectly reasonable to think that the life-giving God would not let death have the last word?

But we need to ask our 'why' question again. Why did he need to rise again from the dead? What was the point?

As we know, death is in every respect the result of sin. One always follows the other, even as far back as the garden of Eden. So if Jesus *did* deal properly with sin in his death, if he took on the wrath and judgement of God, and sin was finished with once and for all, then what should we expect to see? Well, the opposite of death—which is resurrection.

Jesus was fully dead and came back to life again. This is the cause of endless celebration for Christians. Not least because of what it means for his followers. The apostle Paul tells us that Jesus' resurrection was the forerunner to the resurrection of all Christian people. Just as Jesus rose from the dead, then one day they too will rise with resurrection bodies (1 Corinthians 15:20-23). The apostle Paul actually makes a direct comparison of Adam and Jesus—just as Adam's actions led to death for all humanity, so too can Jesus' actions (his dying on the cross and then rising again) lead to eternal life for anyone who will take it. Paul says: "For as in Adam all die, so in Christ all will be made alive" (1 Corinthians 15:22).

And since Jesus came back to life again, we can be sure there is really life after death. There is more to life than the here and now; there is more to come. We can be sure of what we perhaps had an inkling of all along—that inkling that there is more to life than meets the eye; there is a greater purpose; there is a deep soul-drenching satisfaction that frees us from our earthly longing. Did you know, the Bible even tells us that God placed this inkling for something more in our hearts, right from the very beginning? In Ecclesiastes 3:11 God tells us that he has "set eternity in the human heart".

We knew we were made for more, and now we know *what* we were made for. Eternal, resurrected life with Jesus. It's a reality we can be confident in—a reality with a loving, personal God.

10
Jesus the King

In our world today, kings and queens are often thought of as something from ages past. But since Jesus' death and resurrection, we read of Jesus being the true king, the ultimate ruler of God's world, even today. The apostle Paul gives an excellent summary of all we've talked about so far—how Jesus, although he was fully God, humbled himself, even to the point of death. But now he's been raised and God has elevated him to the highest place. He rules over God's world. Have a look at what Paul says:

> [Jesus], being in very nature God,
>   did not consider equality with God something to
>   be used to his own advantage;
> rather, he made himself nothing
>   by taking the very nature of a servant,
>   being made in human likeness.
> And being found in appearance as a man,

he humbled himself
by becoming obedient to death—
even death on a cross!

Therefore God exalted him to the highest place
and gave him the name that is above every name,
that at the name of Jesus every knee should bow,
in heaven and on earth and under the earth,
and every tongue acknowledge that Jesus Christ is Lord,
to the glory of God the Father. (Philippians 2:6-11)

It's because of this that we need to be careful of continued rebellion against the rule of Jesus. We are in a no-win situation if we continue to oppose him. Jesus himself will be our judge on the day of judgement. Paul explained it like this:

…he [God] commands all people everywhere to repent. For he has set a day when he will judge the world with justice by the man he has appointed. He has given proof of this to everyone by raising him from the dead. (Acts 17:30-31)

This present world order won't go on forever. God has chosen a day when history will end. And on that day Jesus will return to earth. But this time he won't come as a tiny, vulnerable baby. This time he will come in triumph and power. It will be clear to *all people* that he is indeed the king of God's world. At this appointed time, Jesus will judge each and every person—those living and those who have already died—according to how we have treated him. Then he will set up a new heaven and a new earth where evil will be abolished forever, and goodness and righteousness will prevail.

It's in this amazing new earth that God's people will live *forever*! Here there will be no more sickness, suffering, evil or pain. No corruption or injustice. No more tears, anxieties or tensions. No more longings for more. Just pure delight, and perfect fulfilment. The Bible even tells us that God will comfort us like a mother comforts her child (Isaiah 66:13). He will personally wipe away our tears and replace them with such incredible joy.

The Bible paints a vivid picture of the amazing beauty that will be in this new earth. Look at this image given in the book of Isaiah—such harmony and peace await God's people in the new creation!

> The cow will feed with the bear,
>> their young will lie down together,
>> and the lion will eat straw like the ox.
> The infant will play near the cobra's den,
>> and the young child will put its hand into the
>>> viper's nest.
> They will neither harm nor destroy…
> for the earth will be filled with the knowledge of
>> the LORD
>> as the waters cover the sea. (Isaiah 11:7-9)

What a delightful image. Can you even imagine a cow feeding alongside a bear, or an infant playing with a snake and there being no threat? It's pretty mind boggling! And do you see the reason why there is such harmony and peace in this new world? It's because this new earth is "filled with the knowledge of the LORD". It's because God himself will now dwell with his people that this new world will be a place of such delight and harmony. We jump to the very end of the Bible to get this crystal clear picture of the promised world to come:

> "Look! God's dwelling place is now among the people, and he will dwell with them. They will be his people, and God himself will be with them and be their God." (Revelation 21:3)

Does this remind you of anything? This is just what life was like, back in the garden of Eden. Before sin entered the world, the earth was full of the knowledge of the Lord—in fact, up until they first sinned, all Adam and Eve knew was the goodness of God. And because Jesus has overcome the barrier of sin that separated us, God will once again live among his people. So we can think about this new world as a return to Eden—a return to life as it was meant to be. This is the life you were made for!

Why hasn't Jesus returned?

But if our current world is in such a mess, why hasn't Jesus brought in this new creation yet? If the new creation is so good, why does he keep us waiting in this world which is full of sickness, suffering and corruption?

God certainly cares about his people and he cares about his world. And it's actually for this reason that Jesus has delayed his return. The apostle Peter explains why:

> The Lord is not slow in keeping his promise, as some understand slowness. Instead he is patient with you, not wanting anyone to perish, but everyone to come to repentance. (2 Peter 3:9)

Jesus has delayed his return so that you and I have time to come back to God before the day of judgement, before it's too late. God longs for us to come to him. He longs for us to return the love he's shown to us.

But it isn't rocket science to question that if the Bible is true, if Jesus is the only way to restored relationship with God, what happens to all those who are unwilling to commit to Jesus?

This brings us to the oh-so-popular topic of hell, which we've already touched on a little in this book—although we haven't yet used the word. Even writing the word makes me a little anxious. It's a thing we just don't want to talk about. To avoid it would make for a much more palatable meal to present in a book like this. But then I wouldn't be giving you the full picture. We need to understand heaven *and* hell because we are told of these *two* places.

For those who continue to reject God, they face an eternity without him, cut off from his presence forever. This is what the Bible means by hell. Just as an eternity in God's presence is unimaginably delightful, the Bible describes an eternity *without* God as something unimaginably awful.

It may surprise you to find out that the person who spoke most about the existence of hell was Jesus himself. He didn't hold back with his description and that's because he wants people to know where they are heading if they reject his free offer of salvation.

Because God is the source of all good things, and hell is a place without God's presence, there will be *no* good thing in hell. There will be no limits to evil. According to Jesus, hell is a place of eternal torment, a lake of fire where people are punished forever for their rejection of him (Revelation 14:9-11;

20:10; 14-15). Jesus tells us that more than anything we are to fear hell (Matthew 10:28).

I've heard people say, "I might go to hell but all my friends will be there with me". But according to the Bible this idea is wrong. Yes, your friends may be there but friendship is a *good* thing, so it won't exist in hell. The Bible tells that all a person can think about in hell is their pain and anguish.

Friend, as you digest this biblical truth about the reality of hell, it may taste bitter in your mouth. I understand—it's also something I've struggled with. But God is just and he must punish sin. And this is punishment each of us deserves. Indeed, it's the punishment we invite when we say 'Go away, God'. Yet God in his mercy has offered us a way out.

I know this is direct, but it's out of love and concern that I tell you these things. Please, I urge you to come to Jesus now and receive forgiveness while you can still can. Come to the gentle Saviour who spoke so tenderly to the sinful, needy people he met during his lifetime. He will graciously greet you and welcome you into his arms.

11

So what about you?

Do you ever have salespeople come to your door to try and sell you things? From home insurance to electricity providers and everything in between, if I'm at home during the day and hear an unexpected knock, chances are someone will be presenting me with an offer and will want at least a commitment of money, if not cash right then and there.

Most of the time I can't be bothered with the interruption and I'm pretty sure I won't be interested in what they've got to sell. I've tried a few approaches—the first is to quietly hide, ignoring them, hoping they will go away. Sometimes I open the door but cut them off before they start their speech, telling them I'm not interested, and hopefully saving time for both of us. A third approach is to pretend I'm interested and then let them down gently, which isn't really much fun for either of us. The final approach (which is very rare) is that I act interested, because I actually *am* interested and then I sign on the dotted line.

I think people often have these same approaches to Jesus. If you've read to this point of the book, you will hopefully have a fairly clear understanding of who Jesus is and the claims he makes. But like with a salesperson at the door, this is the point where you have to work out for yourself what you believe—and what you want to do about it.

Have you been hiding from Jesus and from anyone associated with him, hoping that all this talk about religion will simply go away? Or do you take the 'shut down' approach with anyone who tries to talk to you about Christianity? Maybe you prefer the 'I like the idea of Jesus and I believe in God but I don't want to change my life for him' attitude. Or perhaps you've reached the end of this book with a genuine desire to know more.

If you are one of the first three people, I want to say that I'm praying for you. God is offering you a relationship that will meet your greatest need and longing. Can I encourage you to keep thinking about this offer, even if you're not yet ready to accept it? At the end of this book I've listed some other books that I think might be helpful if you want to give this some more thought.

If you are the fourth type of person—someone who now wants a personal relationship with the God who made you— then that relationship with God can be yours. But what does that actually look like?

Saying sorry

I so often have to remind my children to apologize. "Have you said sorry?" is a question that is regularly found on my lips. Yet when *I've* wronged someone, I'm often amazed at how hard it is for me to say sorry! Admitting we are wrong can be a real challenge for some of us. Or maybe you're a person of many 'sorrys' who is constantly apologizing for anything and everything without really thinking through what you're saying. Either way, 'sorry' is something that is hard to truly mean.

We have all treated God badly. We have ignored him, or turned to him only when we are really desperate, treating him like a genie in a bottle, or else we have simply rebelled in open hostility. So we need to apologize to God for the way we have treated him.

The Bible calls this 'repentance' and it says this is what our response to God should be. Repentance is admitting that I have rebelled against God's rightful rule over my life. But it's more than just feeling sorry. It's a change of mind towards God and declaring my intention to live with God as my rightful ruler from now on, to the best of my ability.

A matter of faith

As well as repenting before God, the Bible also calls us to put our faith in Jesus as our Saviour and Lord. Faith is quite a vague word these days but when the Bible talks about faith it really just means trust. We're to trust that Jesus died and rose back to life for sinners, so that we can be forgiven (Romans 4:25).

Trusting in Jesus is a life-altering decision with eternal consequences. The person who puts their faith in what Jesus has done for them must fully abandon the trust they formerly had in themselves. Before coming to Jesus they may have felt they were pretty good and actually doing all right at this thing called life. Like me, they may have reveled in the praise people gave them, which only served to reaffirm their belief that they were actually pretty good people.

But after hearing the truth about God in the Bible, we need to make a U-turn. Now we realize that we are only acceptable to God because of Jesus. We transfer our trust from ourselves to Jesus. We realize we were utterly deluded to put our trust in our own good deeds to get us to heaven.

I have a question for you, and your answer will show exactly where your trust (faith) is placed. If you were to die today and stood in the presence of God and he said to you, "Why should I let you into my heaven?", what would you answer? If your answer begins "Because I…", then your trust is placed in yourself. But the person who has responded to God in repentance and faith would answer, "Because Jesus died and rose again for me". Their confidence and trust is in Jesus.

We don't have to worry about the *amount* of faith we have, though. It's all about *who* our faith is in. Think back to the story of the bleeding woman. When Jesus calls her out of the crowd, he lifts up this desperate woman as an example of what it means to have faith in Jesus.

Here is a woman who is *so* aware of her need and who knows only Jesus can meet it. She knows she can't save herself—she's tried that. She knows that without Jesus she will continue to be unclean, and will keep on living in relational isolation. And so she comes to him with empty-handed trust and grasps hold of Jesus.

Jesus tells her that her faith in *him* has healed her. Her faith is tentative at first, and it's desperate. It's not impressive in any way. But it's enough to heal her, because it's placed in the right person. She trusted in *Jesus* as the only one who can save her.

This woman is an example to the crowd that surrounded Jesus, and she is an example to us. This is how Jesus says we must relate to him. And maybe that makes you a little uncomfortable. Because I, for one, like to think that I'm not quite as desperate as the bleeding woman. Although I might not be perfect, I like to think that I've got it a bit more together. I'm not in *that* much need of help. I pull out my life résumé and soothe myself that actually I have done some pretty great things. I'm not like her at all.

But then I stop and remember that before God, we actually are desperate. The Bible even tells us that all our good deeds are like smelly bloodstained rags compared to the holy perfection God requires (see Isaiah 64:6). This seems pretty harsh, but it's a sobering realty isn't it?

When it comes to sin though, all of us are completely dependent on God to save us. The Bible says it's like we're trapped and sinking in a clay bog (Psalm 40:2). We are stuck in our sin and just can't set ourselves free. Nothing and no-one can save us apart from God. Not giving money to the Red Cross, not getting an A+ in parenting, not having a stellar career, not even our religious activities. We absolutely need Jesus every bit as much as the bleeding woman did.

So my question is: like the bleeding woman, will you reach out to Jesus in faith?

If you do, you can be sure that Jesus will respond with the same grace and compassion that he showed to her. Remember how tenderly he spoke to her? "Daughter, your faith has healed you. Go in peace." Those very words can be true for you too.

There's a cost

Any savvy marketing person would tell me to stop right there. But there is more to say, because following Jesus isn't a popular choice. It isn't easy; it has a cost.

Like we've already talked about, repentance means making a U-turn in our lives, turning from our selfishness back towards God. Choosing to follow Jesus means dislodging all the things that have, until now, occupied the place of God in your life. For we have *all* filled our longings for more with something other than God, and in most cases we have actually honoured that thing in a way that only God deserves. In most cases, we have let that thing (or things) be the driving force of our lives.

You might need to take some time to think about what or who has been the ruler of your life, that thing that you've put in God's place. It could be your career, or your children, or your marriage or your friends, or your popularity, or your desire to have a comfortable life, or your desire for financial security… you get the idea.

While you're thinking about what it might be for you, let me tell you about a man who we read about in Luke 18, who had been filling his longing for more with the wrong thing. For him, his false 'god' was money. When Jesus confronts this man, he makes an absolute claim on his life.

The Bible doesn't actually tell us the name of this man, simply that he was young, rich and a ruler. He was a man who had it *all*. In many ways, he lived the dream life. He was successful and wealthy, but he didn't sleep around or get drunk or cheat others. He cared about doing the right thing.

This man comes to Jesus, asking the question we all want

answered: "what must *I* do to inherit eternal life?" (Luke 18:18). Jesus answers by making a list of things people think they need to do to be good enough: do not commit adultery, do not murder, do not steal, do not lie, honour your father and mother. This makes the man exceedingly happy because he thinks he's lived a good life. Relieved and perhaps a little proud, he replies "All these [commandments] I have kept since I was a boy". But Jesus goes on and says, "You still lack one thing. Sell everything you have and give to the poor, and you will have treasure in heaven. Then come, follow me" (Luke 18:22).

This was bad news for the man, because this was the one thing he could not do. His reaction is understandable on one level. Like him, we are trained from the earliest of ages to believe that wealth brings security. This rich ruler loved his wealth and loved the power and enjoyment it brought him.

But Jesus showed this man that only God could occupy the number one spot in his life. Jesus had to come first, even above the money that he thought would bring him security. The rich man wasn't willing to give up his most prized possession for Jesus, though. This was *too* great a price to pay for eternal life. He chose comfort and power and security on this earth, rather than looking at the forever life to come.

Jesus doesn't put a condition on the offer of salvation. Remember, we are saved by nothing other than Jesus' death and resurrection. Nothing we *do* will save us. For us, being saved is impossible, but it's not impossible for God (Luke 18:26-27). It's only in accepting the saving hand that God offers that we have eternal life.

But Jesus did ask this man to put him above his finances in response to knowing who God is and all that he has done for his people. And he asks us to do the same.

Jesus wants the number one place in our life; above our wealth, above our accolades, above what our partner or family member or friend thinks. You can't fit Jesus in around all the other important facets of your life. He is either number one, or nothing at all.

That doesn't mean neglecting responsibilities, like earning money to support yourself and your family, and caring for others.[7] Those are good things. But it does mean re-arranging every single responsibility in light of Jesus now being at the centre of your world.

Who or what currently has the tightest hold of your heart?

God wants *all* of you. And he went to such extraordinary lengths to show you this—his Son died for sinful people like you and me, even people who struggle to make Jesus number one.

It's worth it

Like any bargain-hunter, I'm always weighing up cost versus reward. As my husband always reminds me, even with a very discounted item (win!) I am still spending money. So, when I see an item of clothing for sale that I'd love, I still try to work out whether wearing that dress will be worth parting with my cash.

I imagine you are thinking through whether the reward outweighs the cost when it comes to following Jesus. Let

---

7   The Bible is clear that caring for our parents and children is really important and actually there are serious consequences for those who don't provide for their relatives. See 1 Timothy 5:8 "Anyone who does not provide for their relatives, and especially for their own household, has denied the faith and is worse than an unbeliever".

me assure you that with Jesus, although the cost is high, the reward is far greater. It is *so* worth following Jesus.

First of all, just remember the amazing promise of the world to come for all who put their trust in Jesus. You are headed for a perfect world in relationship with the perfect God who made you.

We don't like thinking about death much in our culture, but don't let that cause you to overlook the certainty of it. We will all die, and you can't take anything with you then—not your money, not even your loved ones. I think of the ancient Egyptians, burying treasure in the pyramids with their pharaohs, hoping against hope that this would help the pharaoh have a good life after death. But this was an empty hope—the pyramids have been opened, and the corpses found alongside the buried treasure. The Bible reminds us again and again not to store up our treasures on earth, because these things won't last into the next life.

So why not invest in the one thing that outlasts death? Jesus is the one person who will be with you through this life and into the next, and in that new world he promises you pleasure beyond your imagining—for all eternity. To me it seems like a no-brainer, even if it means giving up everything now. But the benefits are not just in the next life; there are so many benefits to following Jesus *right now*.

Look at the extraordinary promise Jesus gives after speaking with the rich man who refuses to give up his wealth:

> "Truly I tell you… no-one who has left home or
> wife or brothers or sisters or parents or children for
> the sake of the kingdom of God will fail to receive
> *many times as much in this age*, and in the age to come
> eternal life." (Luke 18:29-30)

The great paradox of the Christian life is that as you give up the things you once held dear for Jesus, you gain back a hundredfold *in this life*, as well as the next. The benefits of following Jesus are not just realized in the world to come. We don't have to grit our teeth and bear it until we get to heaven. Jesus actually offers life *in all its fullness* right now (John 10:10).

Even as we wait for the world to come, there is true joy, fulfilment and meaning to be had as we live each day with Jesus. So I want to finish this book by telling you about some of the amazing joys of knowing Jesus while we wait for his return. This is what it means to live the life you were made for in the here and now.

12
Living the life you were made for

You're never alone

When I first held my daughter in my arms, moments after she'd been delivered, I was shell-shocked. My body had just been through the most traumatic experience and I was overcome with emotions and anxiety. After the midwife helped us to our room, she said goodnight and told us to call her if we needed anything. I couldn't believe that she'd left us! Where was the guidebook? Why on earth was I being trusted to do this enormously important job without someone to coach me every step along the way?

It's a bit like life, isn't it? No-one gives us a step-by-step manual on how to really live it. Instead we often muddle through, with the saying 'fake it until you make it' echoing in our minds. Yet for people who follow Jesus, life is different.

Before Jesus' death, he explained to his closest followers that he would soon be going away. They must have felt real anxiety. How would they do life now, without Jesus physically walking beside them, teaching them, talking with them? But Jesus promised them that they wouldn't be left alone. He would send his Spirit to come and live with them. The Holy Spirit is sometimes referred to in the Bible as the "Spirit of Jesus" (Philippians 1:19), the "Holy Spirit" (Luke 11:13), or just the "Spirit" (Philippians 2:1).

The Bible tells us that this same Spirit dwells in *all* of God's people. It's the Spirit who gives us eyes to see Jesus for who he really is, and to trust that God's words are true. If you trust in Jesus, it's because of the Holy Spirit's work in you. And if you trust in Jesus, it means God's own Spirit has come to permanently live in you. God will never leave you to navigate life alone. There'll never be a situation where you need to think of yourself as a lone ranger. As Jesus himself said, "Surely I will be with you always, to the very end of the age" (Matthew 28:20).

One of the great benefits of a true relationship with Jesus is the experience of knowing that I am cared for, loved, and known by him. Sometimes I find I'm misunderstood, even by those I'm closest to. It's enormously comforting to know that I am never misunderstood or ignored by Jesus. He is never too caught up in other business to care about me. The Bible describes Jesus as a shepherd, lovingly and tenderly caring for his sheep, knowing each one of them by name and never, ever leaving them. He goes ahead of them, leading and guiding them to where they need to be (John 10:3-4). How wonderful that even though I've rebelled against God, he is still utterly committed to caring for me every moment of every day, all because of Jesus.

You're a new person

When I graduated from my teaching degree, I had a newfound confidence in my teaching abilities. That piece of paper meant that the Teaching Institute of New South Wales trusted me to teach teenagers what they needed to know about English and Art. My status changed from student to teacher. That piece of paper allowed me to enter a classroom as a different person. Sure, I was still the same Emily, yet I was also transforming into a new Emily—Emily the teacher.

In a similar yet so much more significant way, when I repent of my sin and trust Jesus to be Saviour of my life, a profound change happens. God creates a new person, or as the Bible puts it, gives me a new 'heart' that no longer rebels against him. So dramatic is the change that a person is said to be 'born again' as God's own child (John 3:3).

This is the work of the Holy Spirit. As he sweeps through my heart, he changes who I am at the core of my being. Not only does the Spirit give me eyes to see Jesus for who he is, he also enables me to live God's way—to do what we could never have done before. He causes my desires to change from being me-centred to Jesus-centred. It's because of the Spirit that I want to become like Jesus and live life as it was really meant to be lived. The result of the work of the Holy Spirit is described like this:

> The fruit of the Spirit is love, joy, peace, forebearance, kindness, goodness, faithfulness, gentleness and self-control. (Galatians 5:22-23)

The moment we become a Christian, the Spirit begins his work of growing these God-like attributes in us, so that we mirror our Saviour. Just as in human families, children often have the same qualities and attributes, so too does God want *his* children to become like him and his perfect Son, Jesus—loving, gracious, patient, kind, good, gentle and self-controlled.

> Follow God's example, therefore, as dearly loved children and walk in the way of love, just as Christ loved us and gave himself up for us as a fragrant offering and sacrifice to God. (Ephesians 5:1-2)

But why, you might ask, are Christians still so *imperfect*? It's true; every Christian has a long way to go before they reach Jesus' standard of perfection. And sometimes Christians can be particularly hypocritical, angry, unloving and unkind. Far from being Christlike, sometimes they can even be less pleasant than people who don't know Jesus. I was recently talking with a friend who was thinking through the idea of God. One thing that has put her off Christianity is actually her interaction with Christians, which is really sad.

But when God begins to create a new person inside the old person—the old self that ignored God and made her own decisions—then the result is a battle. While the Spirit works in you to trust Jesus and to live like him, your old self wants you to return to your old ways. A Christian will always have a conflicting desire of their old and new desires, and this tension will be something we live with until we're in heaven and sin and evil are finally done away with forever.

The longer I live as a Christian, the more I see the battle I'm in and the depth of my own sinfulness. I continue to battle with anger, pride, with comparing myself to others. But if anything, this just causes me to be more thankful to God for the death that he's saved me from. I always need to remember that no matter what happens, my relationship with God isn't dependent on my success as a Christian. I am only acceptable to God because of what Jesus has already done in my place. This brings me to the next benefit of life with Jesus.

You're forgiven

Putting your trust in Jesus means that *you are forgiven*. Jesus, through his death on the cross, has completely paid for his people's sin. We have all done things we shouldn't have, things that we regret. But when we trust in Jesus, it means all of our mistakes—past, present, and future—are nailed to the cross and dealt with before God (Colossians 2:14). Because of the absolute sufficiency of Jesus' sacrifice in our place, there is no room for guilt in the Christian life. You are totally forgiven. God treats you as if you never sinned. When you really let the weight of that sink in, it almost sounds too good to be true. But it really is true!

It brings an immense freedom in life. But we no longer think of freedom as being able to do exactly as we want. The apostle Paul writes about this in the book of Romans. If people are saying, 'Hey, I've been forgiven, I can do whatever I want and there'll be no consequences' then Paul's response is, 'Why would you want to keep living in sin?' Because we've been so generously loved and forgiven by God, we *want* to live to please him—just like children who truly love their parents don't want to deliberately hurt or displease them (Romans 6:15-18).

Sadly, because we're still living in a sinful world, we will continue to mess up, often despite our best intentions. We won't live perfectly until we're in heaven. But when we trust in Jesus, we can be totally sure of our status as forgiven children. We're secure and nothing can change that. Nothing can separate us from the love of God that is ours because of Jesus (Romans 8:39).

You don't need to fear death

We've touched on this one already, but it's so good that I have to come back to it! In our society I think the thing we fear most is death. That's why no-one wants to talk about it. We like to think we can control most things in life, especially if we have money to spare. But when it comes to death, no-one can escape it. We see it coming with signs of ageing on our bodies, but sometimes it comes unannounced—an unexpected diagnosis, a car accident, a sudden death or miscarriage. All of it is beyond our control, and if we pause to acknowledge that, surely each one of us would be fearful. Death robs everything of meaning. We live and we work and we invest in relationships, but to what end? Death comes along and snatches everything away.

At the start of this year, my father woke up one morning with loss of movement down one side of his body. Although doctors initially thought he'd had a stroke, we soon found out he had a lesion on his brain, most probably an aggressive tumour. As we waited for further tests to confirm his diagnosis, I found out that dad was likely not to make my youngest daughter's fifth birthday. It was a time of confronting death head-on, which gave life a bittersweet clarity.

For the follower of Jesus however, there is no need to

fear death. My dad is someone who trusts in Jesus and even as he faced a sooner than expected death, he knew the certainty of salvation and that the promise of the life to come far surpasses anything this world has to offer. In fact, the Bible tells us that life after death—an eternal life in the presence of God—is actually the life we were made for. So far from fearing death, we can actually *look forward* to the day when the life we were made for is fully realized—the day when we meet God face to face. My dad ended up being diagnosed with a rare brain infection that was treated with antibiotics, but we know today, just as we knew then, that "to live is [for] Christ and to die is *gain*" (Philippians 1:21). Those were the words of the apostle Paul as he faced a death sentence for following Jesus. Such was his confidence in the goodness of eternal life with God that he actually spoke about leaving this earthly life as *gain*. He knew the best was yet to come.

Similarly, in the book of Acts we read about a man named Stephen who was the first Christian to be murdered for his belief that Jesus was the saving Son of God. The religious leaders of the day were so offended by his beliefs (and the fact that he shared them so openly) that they stoned him to death. I can't even imagine the physical pain he endured as the rocks pierced his flesh and broke his bones, let alone the hateful words of his attackers that would have sliced into his heart and mind. Yet the Bible tells us that Stephen was completely at peace even as he was being killed. Before they stoned him, God gave him a vision of the splendour he was about to enter, showing him the risen Jesus ruling over the new creation. The pummelling rocks and the hateful words must have seemed inconsequential compared to his future certainty of being with God in heaven (Acts 7:54-60).

You can know God more and more

When we come to trust in Jesus, we don't have to pass a Bible-knowledge test. Like the bleeding woman, we just have to put our faith in the right person. The moment we trust in Jesus, no matter the extent of our knowledge of him, we can be sure that we're right with God.

But it's natural we now want to know more about the God who made us and saved us. God actually invites us to know him more and more intimately, because he's our Father.

I started this book by saying that I truly knew the one true God because I've read the words he's given us. Growing in knowledge of God through his word is actually a delight! King David in the Old Testament section of the Bible even described God's words as being sweeter than honey to his lips (Psalm 119:103).

God's words make sense of the mess of this world and give guidance, purpose and meaning. As we learn more about God, we learn more about ourselves and our world. Even though these words were written thousands of years ago, because they come from God they are also eternal. God does not change and neither does the nature of humanity. The thing I find so amazing about God's word is that as we read the pages of biblical history we see that people don't really change all that much! People throughout all ages have sought love and satisfaction in all the wrong places, but God—our good and gracious creator—tells us what will bring us lasting joy. Above all, the Bible is where God makes known his amazing plan of salvation through Jesus.

The Bible is the ultimate guidebook for life. It may not answer every single question we have, but it contains all that we need to know to navigate life on earth while we wait for heaven (2 Peter 1:3). As new ideas ebb and flow, as technology advances, we can keep coming back to God's word, testing everything against these timeless truths. This is such a relief in a confusing world. The Bible doesn't change—God's word "endures forever" (1 Peter 1:25).

A few years ago I had to give up coffee for health reasons, and since then I've become a tea fanatic. One thing I've learned about tea is that the longer the tealeaves are infused in the pot or cup, the stronger the tea becomes. In some ways, our minds are like a fresh cup of hot water, and the more time we spend thinking about certain things, the more our lives change to become like that thing. When we spend time reading and learning from God's word, our thinking also changes to become more in line with God's thinking, which can only be a good thing. After all, God wants his children to become more and more like him.

Psalm 119 is a beautiful poem about God's word, likening it to a light in the darkness, helping us understand more of who God is and how to live in light of that. The writer says: "Your word is a lamp for my feet, a light on my path… The unfolding of your words gives light; it gives understanding to the simple" (Psalm 119:105, 130).

When Jesus returns, the Bible tells us we will know God fully (1 Corinthians 13:12). What an exciting thought! But in the meantime we will never exhaust the riches of the Bible. We can truly spend our whole lives getting to know God, and what an amazing thing that is.

God hears you

It seems that whenever a major tragedy happens, people turn to prayer. When the Paris terrorist attacks happened in 2015, the #PrayforParis hashtag became a global phenomenon on social media. On one level this was a powerful way for people around the world to show support for the Parisian victims. Yet it also makes me think that there's a lot of confusion about what prayer really is.

The Bible tells us that prayer is, quite simply, talking to the one true God. It's the great privilege of those who have a restored relationship with God. As we already know, our sin has created a separation between humanity and God. Without trusting in Jesus, this chasm simply means that we can't talk to God. But through his death and resurrection, Jesus opened up the way for us to know God, and now those who trust in Jesus can speak to God directly. And we can talk to him not as some distant aunt who gets a Christmas card every few years, but as a child talking to their loving Father.

My husband is a teacher at the school where our daughter just completed her first year of kindergarten. Although Dave is a teacher at the school, our daughter always has access to him there, because he is her father. If she needs to give him a cuddle, she can go to him. If she is feeling upset about friendships, she can chat with him. This is true of our relationship with God—we can approach God and speak to him anytime and anywhere. We can chat about the tiny details of our lives or the mammoth decisions we need to make. Even as I write this, I am reminded just how amazing that privilege is! The God who flung stars into space, who designed the atmosphere, who made the giant elephant and the tiny grasshopper and everything in between, also hears my less-than-eloquent prayers. He welcomes me to come to him and he lovingly listens and responds.

God isn't like a cosmic Santa Clause though. We don't go to him with our gift list, telling him what we want and when we want it. As we remember who God is, we'll also remember it's not our job to tell God what he should do! God is all-powerful, all-knowing and ever-present. So we should come to him humbly, recognizing who he is and trusting he will always do what's best. I really love this passage from the Bible that reminds me how much greater God's thoughts are than mine:

> "For my thoughts are not your thoughts,
>   neither are your ways my ways", declares the LORD.
> "As the heavens are higher than the earth,
>   so are my ways higher than your ways
>   and my thoughts than your thoughts."
> (Isaiah 55:8-9)

These verses show me that God may answer my prayers differently to what I ask or expect, or he may decide that the answer to my request is 'no'. But I can rest in the knowledge that he is always working to make me more like Jesus. While he doesn't promise a storm-free life, he does promise to carry me through the storms that come my way.

You're part of a new family

As I was chatting with some women recently about their views on Jesus, one lovely lady mentioned that she was struck by the community Christians have. You've probably heard the oft-quoted saying, 'It takes a village to raise a child'. But you can actually finish that saying with lots of different tasks, not just raising a child. Many jobs require a team of people to get them done well.

Well, it's no different when it comes to following Jesus, and this is yet another joy of the Christian life. God intends for us to live our life with him in community with others who also know him. In contrast to our culture today, the life you were made for is not an individualistic one. It's one that's deeply connected to others who share your core identity.

The Bible says that because we belong to Jesus, we should gather together with others who belong to Jesus. As Christians, we are the children of God. So when we meet with our fellow Christians we are gathering as family, as brothers and sisters who call the one true God 'Father'. So when you become a Christian you not only come to know God, you gain a whole new family. And as in human families, you have no choice about who your brothers and sisters are! Like any family, there are ups and downs, but overall it is a wonderful thing to be part of. The joy of being part of this family is that you have a shared purpose in life to love and serve Jesus.

In community we love one another, share in the joys and struggles of life, grow together and say the hard things that sometimes need to be said. We call our Christian community 'church'. Although it's come to mean different things over the centuries, the original word 'church' literally meant 'gathering'. In the first century, churches were gatherings of Christians who came together to hear the truth, pray, encourage each other in it, and work together at making Jesus known to their world. This is still what the church should be doing today.

The Bible describes the church as a 'body'. Like a body,

the church is made up of lots of different parts that do lots of different jobs. In church there are people with different personalities, strengths and weaknesses but we all work together for the same goal. I love my church. Had we never been part of our church, we would never have met some of the people who are now dear friends—people who are very different from us and who we'd never get a chance to mix with aside from church. There is such a wonderful range of people. There are school principals and those who have struggled with drug addiction. There are those who are happy speaking up front and others who would much rather have one-to-one conversations. The glue that keeps us all together is Jesus.

The church should be a place of community, of love, of shared life and of encouragement to keep learning and growing in Jesus. After all, it takes a village to grow a Christian!

I recently talked to a friend who had started coming along to church because she enjoyed the community feel and the way the church loved her daughter. While this friend was still learning about Jesus, she found love, acceptance and support from the church community. Here the church was doing exactly what Jesus himself would have done by lovingly welcoming this woman, caring for her and inviting her to come and know her creator personally.

That said, sinful and broken people live inside the church, just as much as they do outside the church. Again, while we are this side of heaven, the church will always be a far from perfect place. But the church is actually an imperfect picture of the perfect world to come, when all of God's family are gathered around him in heaven, living together in perfect unity and praising God in all we do. Church gives us a real taste of the future life we were made for.

You can live with purpose

When you know Jesus, you have a new way of seeing the world. I don't need to ask 'Is this all there is?', because I know for certain there is more, and I know what that 'more' is.

The world tells us that to reach our potential we need to be our best selves, live out our dreams, carve out our own unique path. That's what real life is about.

I hope I've shown that the Bible defines our purpose in a radically different way. My purpose doesn't depend on me. In fact, it actually depends on my dying to myself—my old habits and desires—and giving my life to Jesus.

It's about living each day in submission to God's will, knowing that he cares for me intimately, knowing that he speaks to me in his word, knowing that he hears me when I pray, knowing that I'm saved no matter what. It's about living with the certain hope of a new world to come. It's about meeting with others who share in this same life purpose and as we gather, having a taste of the sheer delight to come when we gather round the throne of our great God in heaven. It doesn't mean not enjoying earthly pleasures of the here and now—things like delicious food, good friendships and lovely holidays. But it means seeing them in light of the world to come, and as generous gifts from a good God rather than something I've earned for myself.

It's also about making these life-changing truths known to others. Not in a pious and 'Bible bashing' kind of way—but in a way that acknowledges the desperately sinful situation of humanity and the acute need of each and every person for a Saviour. God has provided a Saviour by sending his one and only Son. Having come to this realization, how could I not share that with others? Christianity is one beggar telling another beggar where he found bread.

I don't know if you ever think about your personal legacy, but nothing could be more significant than this because it concerns eternity! I honestly can't imagine a greater or more liberating purpose in life. It's not all about me—it's about the God who made me and saved me. It's an all-encompassing purpose that affects lives now and forever.

Two paths

I hope it's clear that, to me at least, it is so worth giving your life to Jesus. We receive treasures in the life to come, but also find jewels in the here and now. Living my life as a follower of Jesus has been the single best decision I have ever made. But only you can make the decision that's before you now (if you've not already made up your mind).

During high school I studied Robert Frost's poem 'The Road Not Taken'. It's quite a nostalgic poem about a traveller coming to a fork in the road and questioning which of two paths to take. The outcome of both is hidden from view, so he has to decide which road to travel down without knowing the end result of either one.

You also have a choice to make. But unlike Frost, who didn't know the outcome of his decision, the Bible tells us clearly the result of each path that's before us. As we know, those who continue on their own way and reject God as ruler stand condemned, facing judgement and eternal separation from God after they die. Yet those who take the road less trodden—the one that's marked by reliance on Jesus' death and resurrection, and submission to him as your ruler—can be sure of God's forgiveness. This road may be harder at times, but it will be infinitely more meaningful and will end in blissfully restored relationship with your Creator God; a return to an even better garden of Eden.

Our lives can be so busy and full of 'things' that we never pause to examine our deepest needs, and our truest and greatest longings are drowned out. Don't be like Eve—so captivated by the seeming pleasures of *this* world that it prevents you seeing the infinite joy offered if you would just raise your eyes and see the bigger picture. I think CS Lewis is right when he says that as we consider the staggering rewards promised by the God of the Bible, our desires are not too strong but too weak. We settle for the short-term 'satisfactions' of life as though that is all there is. We're "like an ignorant child who wants to go on making mud pies in a slum because he cannot imagine what is meant by the offer of a holiday at the sea. We are far too easily pleased."[8]

It turns out we were made for another world, and although we're not there yet there is so much to be gained in following Jesus right now. No-one can love you more or offer you more satisfaction, meaning and purpose, both now and eternally. Please, give up living for yourself and turn to Jesus. We really were made for more.

8   CS Lewis, *The Weight of Glory and Other Addresses*, HarperOne, New York, 2011, p. 26.

PS
Some next steps

I said at the beginning of the book that you may end up with more questions than you started with. That is a good thing! I want to suggest some next steps if you're still thinking things through. Even if you think at this stage this is not for you, I'd urge you to give Jesus a proper hearing and to do some more investigation before you make up your mind.

If you want to find out more

If you've got questions you need answered before making a decision about Jesus, I'd encourage you to talk to a Christian friend. The majority of us Christians (probably including the person who gave you this book!) are eagerly waiting for you to ask *us* questions so that we can talk more openly about our relationship with God. I, for one, can sometimes be unsure about talking about God, not wanting to be overbearing. But when you ask *us* questions, it usually helps kick that stage fright right out the door.

I'd really encourage you to read the Bible for yourself to find answers to your questions. A good place to start would be with one of the Gospels—Matthew, Mark, Luke or John. Here you can read about the life of Jesus from people who witnessed it. If you're unsure how to read the Bible, again, ask a Christian friend or else try to get hold of an excellent little book called *The Book of Books* by Geoff Robson, which explains how to read the Bible for yourself. It's especially helpful for people who have never read the Bible before. The main thing to know is that the Bible is divided into 66 smaller books, which are each divided into chapters (the big numbers) like any other book. Each chapter then has verses (the little numbers) that help us work out which sentence we are reading from. I'd recommend using a modern translation like the New International Version, the English Standard Version or the Christian Standard Bible. If you don't have a physical Bible, you can easily read the Bible online at www.biblegateway.com.

Here are some other books you might find helpful as you think more about what it means to be a Christian:[9]

On the Christian life
John Chapman, *A Fresh Start* (Matthias Media)
Paul Grimmond, *Right Side Up* (Matthias Media)

---

9   Matthias Media titles are available from www.matthiasmedia.com. Crossway titles are available from www.crossway.org.

On Jesus
Greg Gilbert, *Who is Jesus?* (Crossway)

On the reliability of the Bible
Andrew Errington, *Can we trust what the Gospels say about Jesus?* (Matthias Media)
Kevin DeYoung, *Taking God At His Word* (Crossway)

Reasons for belief
Timothy Keller, *The Reason for God: Belief in an age of scepticism* (Crossway)
John Dickson, *If I were God I'd end all the pain* (Matthias Media)
John Dickson, *If I were God I'd make myself clearer* (Matthias Media)

If you've decided to follow Jesus

If you've decided you want to live with Jesus as your king, the next step is simply to talk to God about it and
- admit to God you've rebelled against him
- ask for his forgiveness
- ask for his help to make a fresh start as a follower of Jesus.

If you've prayed those things to God, you may not feel any differently, but in reality *everything* has changed. If you trust in Jesus, you are God's child and your status for all eternity has been secured. Tell a Christian friend, if you can, and they can help you to know what to do next. A great thing to do is to find a church that teaches God's word so you can meet other people who follow Jesus, and be encouraged to grow in your relationship with him.

It's been a joy and privilege to share this news about Jesus with you, and if you've decided to follow him, that is the best possible news. While I may never meet you in this life, I look forward to rejoicing with you in heaven, in the presence of our great God who saved us and made us his own.

Some people to thank

I wrote this book because of one lady who was brave enough to share how hard life had been for her. As she poured out her heart, sharing how much pain certain relationships had caused her, I wanted to talk with her about the hope and healing that Jesus brings. I realized how wonderful it would be to have a book that explained how the most significant relationship we can have, the only one that can meet our greatest needs and longings, is with the God who created us to seek him. I couldn't find one, so felt burdened to write it. I'm thankful to this woman for her willingness to be vulnerable and honest about her desire for more.

I'd like to thank all those who helped make this project possible. To those at Matthias Media—Ian, Emma and my editor Kirsten—and Tara Smith, this book wouldn't have come about without your encouragement, skill and excitement. Kirsten, you are a delight to work with and an answer to prayer. Jono and Sarah, thank you for your passion for *Made for More* to find a home with Matthias Media. Anne, thanks for your early encouragement to keep going. To the ladies in my Bible studies past and present—and especially Rhonda, Beate, Mel, Courtney, Elly and Katrina—thank you for praying and encouraging me each week to share Jesus. Pastor Trent and Fiona, thank you for your enthusiasm for making Jesus known and your encouragement to refine my gifts for God's glory. Ngaire, Nat and Liv, thanks for praying, encouraging my writing and journeying with me through life.

I'm grateful to my family—for my grandma and grandpa who gave me a love for literature and stories; to Sophie and Lydia, my sisters and best friends, for teaching me about relationships and for listening to the longings of my heart; to my mum and dad for raising me to know and love God. Imogen, Gideon and Esther, you three are the loves of my heart and bring me such joy each day. Dave, I am so grateful for everything you are. You are always the first to read and edit my writing and to give me courage when I need it.

To God, the one who gives life, purpose and meaning. I'm grateful beyond words for your gift of Jesus and for your promise of restored relationship. All glory, honour and power belong to you, now and forever.

Matthias Media is an independent Christian publishing company based in Sydney, Australia. To browse our online catalogue, access samples and free downloads, and find more information about our resources, visit our website:

www.matthiasmedia.com

How to buy our resources

1. Direct from us over the internet:
    – in the US: www.matthiasmedia.com
    – in Australia: www.matthiasmedia.com.au

2. Direct from us by phone: please visit our website for current phone contact information.

3. Through a range of outlets in various parts of the world. Visit **www.matthiasmedia.com/contact** for details about recommended retailers in your part of the world.

4. Trade enquiries can be addressed to:
    – in the US and Canada: sales@matthiasmedia.com
    – in Australia and the rest of the world: sales@matthiasmedia.com.au

About the author

Emily Cobb is a writer and graphic designer based on the North Coast of NSW. She is married to Dave and they have three little children. Emily loves being creative and spending time with people. She especially enjoys thinking and chatting about life's deeper questions and the practicalities of living what she believes (ideally over a cup of tea).